T

Workbook & Journal

For

Dr. Nicole Lepera

HOW TO DO

THE WORK

RECOGNIZE YOUR PATTERNS,

HEAL FROM YOUR PAST

AND CREATE YOUR SELF

CHAPTER ONE

YOU ARE YOUR OWN BEST HEALER

Describe your "feeling stuck moment"

_____

_____

_____

_____

_____

_____

_____

_____

_____

Have you tried therapy or other singular transformative

experiences? Describe how it made you feel

_____

_____

_____

_____

_____

_____

_____

_____

_____

Describe the Mind-Body connection. Do you think the

mind and body are interconnected?

_____

_____

_____

_____

_____

_____

_____

_____

_____

_____

Give a brief explanation of the basic tenets of holistic

psychology

_____

_____

_____

———————————————————————

———————————————————————

———————————————————————

———————————————————————

———————————————————————

———————————————————————

———————————————————————

———————————————————————

———————————————————————

———————————————————————

—————————————————

Have you ever had a period of self-sabotage like Ally?

How can the basic tenets of holistic psychology help you

grow out of it?

———————————————————————

———————————————————————

CHAPTER TWO

THE CONSCIOUS SELF: BECOMING AWARE

Have you had to deal with anxiety? Describe your

experience

_____

_____

_____

_____

_____

_____

_____

_____

"You are not your thought" What does this mean to you?

_____

_____

_____

_____

_____

_____

_____

_____

_____

Looking at the Homeostatic impulse, how have you tried to

break free from it in the past?

_____

_____

_____

_____

_____

_____

CHAPTER THREE

A NEW THEORY OF TRAUMA

The chapter begins with Christine and how her abusive childhood led to her state of disassociation. Have you had any traumatic experience that in your opinion has altered your life? Give a brief detail.

_____

_____

_____

_____

_____

_____

_____

_____

_____

Give a brief detail of trauma acquired during childhood that

stemmed from your childhood conditioning

_____

_____

_____

_____

_____

_____

_____

_____

Give an example of childhood experience you have faced

using the archetype of childhood trauma

ARCHETYPES OF CHILDHOOD TRAUMA	PERSONAL EXPERIENCE
Having a Parent Who Denies Your Reality (A typical example of reality denial occurs when a child, feeling uncomfortable around a relative, tells his mother and is met with a response like "Oh, she's just trying to be nice. You'd better be polite.")	
Having a Parent Who	

Does Not See or Hear You (This mindset was born out of an understanding that the only needs children had were basic, such as food and shelter)	
Having a Parent Who Vicariously Lives Through You or Molds and Shapes You (This type of parent-figure is typically known as a "stage parent"—someone who is overzealous and pushes their child to	

become an actress or a singer to fulfill the parent-figure's own needs for fame, achievement, or attention)	
Having a Parent Who Does Not Model Boundaries (Growing up in homes raised by parent-figures who do not fully understand how to use or maintain their own boundaries, making them unable to model	

appropriate limits for us)	
Having a Parent Who Is Overly Focused on Appearance (It can take the form of commenting about the body or appearance of friends, family, or public figures.)	
Having a Parent Who Cannot Regulate Their Emotions	

(Some parent figure may have projected the overwhelming emotional energy outward, screaming, slamming doors, and throwing things or storming off. For others, the emotions project inward, resulting in some kind of withdrawal)	

How have you coped with your trauma? Give details

_____

_____

_____

_____

_____

_____

_____

_____

_____

If your coping mechanism has been maladaptive, how have
you tried to change it?

_____

_____

_____

_____

_____

_____

CHAPTER FOUR

TRAUMA BODY

What physical health issues have you noticed in relation to your trauma (e.g fainting) and how have you dealt with it in the past?

_____

_____

_____

_____

_____

_____

_____

_____

_____

_____

Have you had to deal with chronic stress? What body

response happens to you?

_____

_____

_____

_____

_____

_____

_____

_____

Hve you had to struggle with an overactive sympathetic

response system (what is known as poor vagal tone)? What

was your experience?

_____

_____

_____

_____

_____

_____

_____

_____

Describe immobilization as another body response to stress

_____

_____

_____

_____

_____

_____

_____

_____

Taking a cue from the book, describe a typical day of

emotional addiction for you

_____

_____

_____

_____

_____

_____

_____

_____

CHAPTER FIVE

MIND-BODY HEALING PRACTICES

What other mind-body healing practices have you tried before this book?

_____

_____

_____

_____

_____

_____

_____

_____

Have you had any previous gut related issues?

_____

_____

_____

_____

_____

Using the gut healing process, how would you apply it your

life?

_____

_____

_____

_____

_____

_____

_____

_____

Using the healing sleep process, how would you apply it to your life?

_____

_____

_____

_____

_____

_____

_____

_____

Using the breathe healing process, how would you apply it to your life?

_____

_____

_____

_____

_____

_____

_____

_____

_____

_____

Using the healing with movement process, how would you

apply it in your life?

_____

_____

_____

_____

_____

_____

_____

_____

Using the healing with play process, how would you apply

it in your life?

_____

_____

_____

_____

_____

_____

_____

CHAPTER SIX

THE POWER OF BELIEF

What previous conditioning have you gotten as a child that has stayed till childhood?

_____

_____

_____

_____

_____

_____

_____

_____

What core belief have you formed that has turned to be a

confirmation bias?

_____

_____

_____

_____

_____

_____

_____

_____

What clues did you pick from your parent figure that has

come to determine how you navigate the world?

_____

_____

_____

_____

_____

_____

_____

_____

_____

How were you treated during childhood in relations to the three basic need of the soul?

To be seen

_____

_____

_____

_____

_____

_____

To be heard

To uniquely express our most authentic Selves

CHAPTER SEVEN

MEET YOUR INNER CHILD

What relationship did you have with your parent-figures
and how has it impacted your present relationship?

_____

_____

_____

_____

_____

_____

_____

_____

Briefly describe the four attachment style? Which one best
describes your childhood?

Give a detailed description of your inner child

_____

_____

_____

_____

_____

_____

_____

_____

_____

_____

CHAPTER EIGHT

EGO STORIES

What are some of the core beliefs you have that have shaped your ego

1. _____

   _____

2. _____

   _____

3. _____

   _____

4. _____

   _____

How does the threat to your ego manifest?

_____

_____

_____

_____

_____

_____

_____

_____

_____

How do you project your ego?

_____

_____

_____

_____

_____

_____

_____

Taking a cue from the 4 steps to do the work with your ego, how would you apply each step to your life?

Step One: Allow Your Ego to Introduce Itself

_____

_____

_____

_____

_____

_____

_____

_____

Step Two: Have a Friendly Encounter with Your Ego

_____

_____

_____

_____

_____

_____

_____

_____

_____

Step Three: Name Your Ego

_____

_____

Step Four: Meet the Activated Ego

_____

_____

_____

_____

_____

How does Ego consciousness work in your life? And what

steps have you taken to curb it?

_____

_____

_____

_____

_____

_____

_____

_____

CHAPTER NINE

TRAUMA BONDS

How has your childhood trauma shaped your present relationships?

_____

_____

_____

_____

_____

_____

_____

_____

_____

What are the common signs you witness in your trauma bonds?

_____

_____

_____

_____

_____

_____

_____

_____

_____

What similar environment to our childhood have we replicated in adulthood?

_____

_____

_____

_____

_____

_____

_____

_____

What trauma bond archetype resonates with you and why?

_____

_____

_____

_____

_____

_____

_____

_____

_____

_____

_____

What steps have you taken to cut off trauma bonds and find

authentic true love?

_____

_____

_____

_____

_____

_____

CHAPTER TEN

BOUNDARIES

How was your boundaries disrespected during childhood?

_____

_____

_____

_____

_____

_____

_____

How has niceness been a barrier to your keeping

boundaries?

_____

_____

_____

_____

_____

_____

There are three categories to boundaries, which category do you fall under? And why?

_____

_____

_____

_____

_____

_____

_____

There are four types of boundaries, how do you relate to each of them?

TYPES OF BOUNDARIES	PERSONAL RELATIONS TO THEM
Physical boundary	
Resource boundary	
Mental/emotional boundary	

How have you had to deal with emotional sharing and dumping?

_____

_____

_____

_____

_____

_____

_____

_____

_____

_____

_____

Using the three steps for setting up boundaries, how do you
intend on setting up boundaries?

Step one: define them

_____

_____

_____

_____

_____

_____

Step two: Begin practice setting the boundary

_____

_____

_____

_____

_____

_____

Step three: Maintain the new boundary

_____

_____

_____

_____

_____

CHAPTER ELEVEN

REPARENTING

Give a brief details of how you were trained growing up and how it has affected your parenting?

_____

_____

_____

_____

_____

_____

_____

_____

_____

_____

_____

_____

What does reparenting process looks like to you?

_____

_____

_____

_____

_____

_____

_____

_____

_____

_____

How do you apply the four pillars of reparenting in our

lives?

Emotional regulation

_____

_____

_____

_____

_____

_____

_____

Discipline

_____

_____

_____

_____

———

Self-care

———

Childlike sense of wonder

_____

_____

_____

_____

_____

How do you deal with loneliness, disappointment and anger

while reparenting?

_____

_____

_____

_____

_____

_____

_____

CHAPTER TWELVE

EMOTIONAL MATURITY

Define emotional maturity as it relates to your life

_____

_____

_____

_____

_____

_____

_____

How do you apply the ninety-seconds rule of emotion to

your life?

_____

_____

_____

_____

_____

_____

_____

_____

_____

How would you use soothing and coping with emotional

distress as a means to coping with emotional stress?

_____

_____

_____

_____

_____

_____

_____

_____

_____

_____

Discuss a few ways you can help cultivate emotional

maturity in children

_____

_____

_____

_____

_____

_____

_____

_____

_____

_____

_____

_____

What method of meditation would you use to help increase

your level of emotional maturity and why?

_____

_____

_____

_____

_____

_____

_____

_____

_____

_____

_____

_____

_____

CHAPTER THIRTEEN

INTERDEPENDENCE

What community have you joined or built to help your

healing journey?

_____

_____

_____

_____

_____

_____

How has this community helped your healing journey? (Be

detailed as much as possible)

_____

_____

_____

_____

_____

_____

_____

_____

_____

_____

_____

_____

_____

In your opinion, what are the merits of being part of a community?

_____

_____

Made in the USA
Monee, IL
07 May 2021